a little brown notebook

Scenes from

Emma

by Jane Austen

Illustrated by Beryl Sanders

M·Q·P

Emma Woodhouse, handsome, clever, and rich, with a comfortable home and happy disposition, seemed to unite some of the best blessings of existence; and had lived nearly twenty-one years in the world with very little to distress or vex her.

Sixteen years had Miss Taylor been in Mr Woodhouse's family, less as a governess than a friend, very fond of both daughters, but particularly of Emma. Between *them* it was more the intimacy of sisters ... the real evils indeed of Emma's situation were the power of having rather too much her own way, and a disposition to think a little too well of herself.

Miss Taylor married ... The event had every promise of happiness for her friend ... there was some satisfaction in considering with what self-denying, generous friendship she had always wished and promoted the match ...

How was she to bear the change? – It was true that her friend was going only half a mile from them; but Emma was aware that great must be the difference between a Mrs Weston only half a mile from them, and a Miss Taylor in the house; and with all her advantages, natural and domestic, she was now in great danger of suffering from intellectual solitude.

Mr Knightley, a sensible man about seven or eight-and-thirty, was not only a very old and intimate friend of the family, but particularly connected with it as the elder brother of Isabella's husband.

Mr Knightley, in fact, was one of the few people who could see faults in Emma Woodhouse, and the only one who ever told her of them ...

'Emma never thinks of herself, if she can do good to others,' rejoined Mr Woodhouse, understanding but in part. 'But, my dear, pray do not make any more matches, they are silly things, and break up one's family circle grievously.'

'Only one more, papa; only for Mr Elton.'

Miss Bates enjoyed a most uncommon degree of popularity for a woman neither young, handsome, rich, nor married ... She had never boasted either beauty or cleverness ... she loved everybody, was interested in everybody's happiness, quick-sighted to everybody's merits; thought herself a most fortunate creature, and surrounded with blessings in such an excellent mother and so many good neighbours and friends, and a home that wanted for nothing.

Miss Smith was a girl of seventeen whom Emma knew very well by sight and had long felt an interest in, on account of her beauty ... she was short, plump and fair, with a fine bloom, blue eyes, light hair, regular features, and a look of great sweetness, and before the end of the evening, Emma was as much pleased with her manners as her person, and quite determined to continue the acquaintance.

Those soft blue eyes and all those natural graces should not be wasted on the inferior society of Highbury and its connections. The acquaintance she had already formed were unworthy of her. The friends from whom she had just parted, though very good sort of people, must be doing her harm.

Emma to Harriet on the subject of Mr Martin: 'for though his sisters, from a superior education, are not to be altogether objected to, it does not follow that he might marry anybody at all fit for you to notice. The misfortune of your birth ought to make you particularly careful as to your associates.'

'... but I would have you so firmly established in good society, as to be independent even of Hartfield and Miss Woodhouse. I want to see you permanently well connected ...'

'Mr Elton is good humoured, cheerful, obliging, and gentle. He seems to me, to be grown particularly gentle of late. I do not know whether he has any design of ingratiating himself with either of us, Harriet, by additional softness, but it strikes me that his manners are softer than they used to be. If he means anything, it must be to please you. Did not I tell you what he said of you the other day?'

Harriet ... had heard, as soon as she got back to Mrs Goddard's, that Mr Martin had been there an hour before, and finding she was not at home, nor particularly expected, had left a little parcel for her from one of his sisters ... on opening this parcel, she had actually found, besides the two songs which she had lent Elizabeth to copy, a letter to herself; and this letter was from him – from Mr Martin – and contained a direct proposal of marriage.

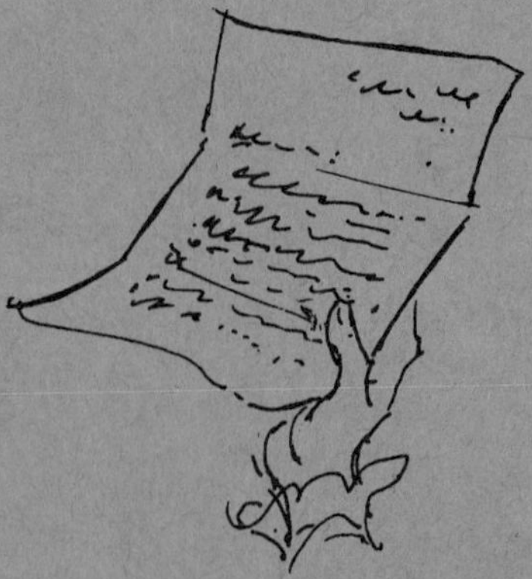

Emma was not sorry to be pressed. She read, and was surprized. The style of the letter was much above her expectation. There were not merely no grammatical errors, but as a composition it would not have disgraced a gentleman, the language, though plain, was strong and unaffected, and the sentiments it conveyed very much to the credit of the writer. It was short, but expressed good sense, warm attachment ... even delicacy of feeling ...

'You think I ought to refuse him then?' said Harriet ...

'You mean to return a favourable answer, I collect.'

'No, I do not; that is, I do not mean – What shall I do? What would you advise me to do? Pray, dear Miss Woodhouse, tell me what I ought to do?'

Mr Knightley actually looked red with surprize and displeasure ...

'You saw her answer! you wrote her answer too. Emma, this is your doing. You persuaded her to refuse him.'

'And if I did, (which, however, I am far from allowing,) I should not feel that I had done wrong.'

' ... Till you chose to turn her into a friend, her mind had not distaste for her own set, nor any ambition beyond it ... You have been no friend to Harriet Smith, Emma.'

'I am very much obliged to you,' said Emma, laughing again. 'If I had set my heart on Mr Elton's marrying Harriet, it would have been very kind to open my eyes; but at present I only want to keep Harriet to myself. I have done with match-making, indeed. I could never hope to equal my own doings at Randalls. I shall leave off while I am well.'

Mr Elton called for a few moments, just to leave a piece of paper on the table containing, as he said, a charade ...

'Take it,' said Emma, smiling, and pushing the paper towards Harriet – 'it is for you. Take your own.'

'My dear Harriet ... Read in comfort to yourself. There can be no doubt of its being written for you and to you.'

'... You and Mr Elton are by situation called together; you belong to one another by every circumstance of your respective homes.'

'I have none of the usual inducements of women to marry. Were I to fall in love, indeed, it would be a different thing! but I never have been in love; it is not my way, or my nature; and I do not think I ever shall. And, without love, I am sure I should be a fool to change such a situation as mine. Fortune I do not want; employment I do not want; consequence I do not want: I believe few married women are half as much mistress of their husband's house, as I am of Hartfield; and never, never could I expect to be so truly beloved and important; so always first and always right in any man's eyes as I am in my father's.'

They walked on. The lane made a slight bend; and when that bend was passed, Mr Elton was immediately in sight ... Mr Elton then turned back to accompany them ... Emma, under pretence of having some alteration to make in the lacing of her half-boot, and stooping down in complete occupation of the footpath, begged them to have the goodness to walk on, and she would follow in half a minute.

The lovers were standing together at one of the windows. It had a most favourable aspect ...

'Cautious, very cautious,' thought Emma; 'he advances inch by inch, and will hazard nothing till he believes himself secure.'

Mr and Mrs John Knightley, from having been longer than usual absent from Surrey, were exciting of course rather more than the usual interest ... Mrs John Knightley was a pretty, elegant little woman, of gentle, quiet manners, and a disposition remarkably amiable and affectionate ... Mr John Knightley was a tall, gentleman-like, and very clever man; rising in his profession, domestic, and respectable in his private character ...

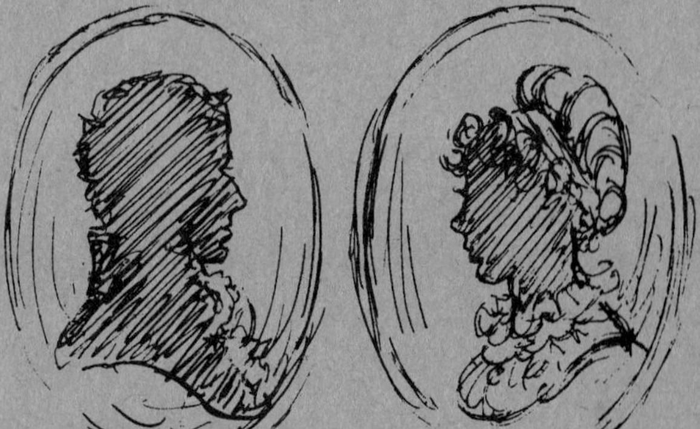

They had not been long seated and composed when Mr Woodhouse, with a melancholy shake of the head and a sigh, called his daughter's attention to the sad change at Hartfield since she had been there last.

'Ah! my dear,' said he, 'poor Miss Taylor – it is a grievous business!'

'Oh! yes, sir,' cried she with ready sympathy, 'how you must miss her! And dear Emma too!'

Mr Knightley was to dine with them ... Emma hoped they might now become friends again ... *she* certainly had not been in the wrong, and he would never own that he had. Concession must be out of the question; but it was time to appear to forget that they had ever quarrelled ...

‘As far as good intentions went, we were both right, and I must say that no effects on my side of the argument have yet proved wrong. I only want to know that Mr Martin is not very, very bitterly disappointed.’

'That sweet, amiable Jane Fairfax!' said Mrs John Knightley – 'It is so long since I have seen her, except now and then for a moment accidentally in town. What happiness it must be to her good old grandmother and excellent aunt, when she comes to visit them ... Jane Fairfax one knows to be so very accomplished and superior!'

They must all dine at Randalls one day ... the evening before this great event ... Harriet had gone home so much indisposed with a cold ... Harriet herself was too ill and low to resist the authority which excluded her from this delightful engagement, though she could not speak of her loss without many tears.

... Mr Elton was to go, and never had his broad handsome face expressed more pleasure than at this moment; never had his smile been stronger, nor his eyes more exulting than when he next looked at her.

'Well,' said she to herself, 'this is most strange! – After I had got him off so well, to chuse to go into company, and leave Harriet ill behind!'

'Yes,' said Mr John Knightley presently, with some slyness, 'he seems to have a great deal of good will towards *you*.'

'Mr Elton in love with me! – What an idea!'

'I do not say it is so; but you will do well to consider whether it is so or not, and to regulate your behaviour accordingly. I think your manners to him encouraging. I speak as a friend, Emma ...'

' ... Mr Elton and I are very good friends, and nothing more.'

Mr Elton, spruce, black, and smiling, was with them instantly. Emma thought with pleasure of some change of subject. Mr Elton was all obligation and cheerfulness; he was so very cheerful in his civilities indeed, that she began to think he must have received a different account of Harriet from what had reached her ...

They walked into Mrs Weston's drawing-room ... Mr Elton was continually obtruding his happy countenance on her (Emma's) notice, and solicitously addressing her upon every occasion.

Now, it so happened that in spite of Emma's resolution of never marrying, there was something in the name, in the idea of Mr Frank Churchill, which always interested her.

Emma found, on being escorted and followed into the second carriage by Mr Elton, that the door was to be lawfully shut on them, and that they were to have a tête-à-tête drive. It would not have been the awkwardness of a moment, it would have been rather a pleasure, previous to the suspicions of this very day ...

Scarcely had they passed the sweep-gate and joined the other carriage, than she found her subject cut up – her hand seized – her attention demanded, and Mr Elton actually making violent love to her: availing himself of the precious opportunity, declaring sentiments which must be already well known, hoping – fearing – adoring – ready to die if she refused him; but flattering himself that his ardent attachment and unequalled love and unexampled passion could not fail of having some effect, and in short, very much resolved on being seriously accepted as soon as possible.

'It is impossible for me to doubt any longer. You have made yourself too clear. Mr Elton, my astonishment is much beyond any thing I can express. After such behaviour, as I have witnessed during the last month, to Miss Smith – such behaviour, as I have been in the daily habit of observing – to be addressing me in this manner – this is an unsteadiness of character, indeed, which I had not supposed possible! Believe me, sir, I am far, very far, from gratified in being the object of such professions.'

'Oh! Miss Woodhouse! who can think of Miss Smith when Miss Woodhouse is near! No, upon my honour, there is no unsteadiness of character ... Everybody has their level: but as for myself, I am not, I think, quite so much at a loss. I need not totally despair of an equal alliance, as to be addressing myself to Miss Smith! – No, madam, my visits to Hartfield have been for yourself only.'

How she could have been so deceived ... She looked back as well as she could; but it was all confusion. She had taken up the idea, she supposed, and made everything bend to it ... Mr Elton was proving himself, in many respects, the very reverse of what she had meant and believed him; proud, assuming, conceited; very full of his own claims, and little concerned about the feelings of others ... he wanted to marry well, and having the arrogance to raise his eyes to her, pretended to be in love ...

The first error and the worst lay at her door. It was foolish, it was wrong, to take so active a part in bringing any two people together. It was adventuring too far, assuming too much, making light of what ought to be serious, a trick of what ought to be simple. She was quite concerned and ashamed, and resolved to do such things no more.

Harriet bore the intelligence very well – blaming nobody – and in every thing testifying such an ingenuousness of disposition and lowly opinion of herself, as must appear with particular advantage at that moment to her friend.

They were just approaching the house where lived Mrs and Miss Bates ...

'Are you expecting Miss Fairfax here soon?'

'Oh, yes; next week.'

'Indeed! – That must be a very great pleasure.'

Jane Fairfax was an orphan, the only child of Mrs Bates's youngest daughter ... by birth she belonged to Highbury: and when at three years old, on losing her mother, she became the property, the charge ... of her grandmother and aunt, there had seemed every probability of her being permanently fixed there ... but the compassionate feelings of a friend of her father gave a change to her destiny ... an offer from Colonel Campbell of undertaking the whole charge of her education.

Emma was sorry ... Why she did not like Jane Fairfax might be a difficult question to answer; Mr Knightley had once told her it was because she saw in her the really accomplished young woman, which she wanted to be ...

Jane Fairfax and Frank Churchill had been at Weymouth at the same time. It was known that they were a little acquainted; but not a syllable of real information could Emma procure as to what he truly was ... Emma could not forgive her.

'I hope every body had a pleasant evening,' said Mr Woodhouse, in his quiet way. 'I had. Once, I felt the fire rather too much; but then I moved back my chair a little, a very little, and it did not disturb me. Miss Bates was very chatty and good-humoured, as she always is, though she speaks rather too quick. However, she is very agreeable, and Mrs Bates too in a different way ...'

Miss Bates and Miss Fairfax walked into the room. Full of thanks and full of news, Miss Bates knew not which to give quickest ... 'Have you heard the news? Mr Elton is going to be married ... a Miss Hawkins – that's all I know. A Miss Hawkins of Bath ...'

Emma, alone with her father, had half her attention wanted by him, while he lamented that young people would be in such a hurry to marry – and to marry strangers too – and the other half she could give to her own view of the subject. It was to herself an amusing and a very welcome piece of news, as proving that Mr Elton could not have suffered long; but she was sorry for Harriet: Harriet must feel it ...

Harriet was one of those, who, having once begun, would be always in love ... had there been no pain to her friend, or reproach to herself, in the waverings of Harriet's mind, Emma would have been amused by its variations.

Human nature is so well disposed towards those who are in interesting situations, that a young person, who either marries or dies, is sure of being kindly spoken of.

A week had not passed since Miss Hawkins's name was first mentioned in Highbury, before she was, by some means or other, discovered to have every recommendation of person and mind; to be handsome, elegant, highly accomplished, and perfectly amiable ... the charming Augusta Hawkins, in addition to all the usual advantages of perfect beauty and merit, was in possession of an independent fortune ...

Mr and Mrs Weston were standing to speak to her.

'Frank comes to-morrow ... he is at Oxford to-day, and he comes for a whole fortnight; I knew it would be so ...'

The Frank Churchill so long talked of, so high in interest, was actually before her – he was presented to her, and she did not think too much had been said in his praise; he was a very good looking young man; height, air, address, all were unexceptionable ... She felt immediately that she should like him; and there was a well-bred ease of manner, and a readiness to talk, which convinced her that he came intending to be acquainted with her, and that acquainted they soon must be.

He was very much pleased with Randalls, thought it a most admirably arranged house, would hardly allow it even to be very small, admired the situation, the walk to Highbury, Highbury itself, Hartfield still more ...

'I have the honour of being acquainted with a neighbour of yours, (turning to Emma,) a lady residing in or near Highbury; a family of the name of Fairfax ...'

'You are acquainted with Miss Jane Fairfax, sir, are you?' said Mr Woodhouse, always the last to make his way in conversation; 'then give me leave to assure you that you will find her a very agreeable young lady. She is staying here on a visit to her grandmamma and aunt, very worthy people; I have known them all my life ...'

The next morning brought Mr Frank Churchill again. He came with Mrs Weston ... Emma was wanting to see him again, and especially to see him in company with Mrs Weston, upon his behaviour to whom her opinion of him was to depend.

Emma's very good opinion of Frank Churchill was a little shaken the following day, by hearing that he was gone off to London, merely to have his hair cut. A sudden freak seemed to have seized him at breakfast, and he had sent for a chaise and set off, intending to return to dinner, but with no more important view that appeared than having his hair cut.

There was nothing to denote him unworthy of the distinguished honour which her imagination had given him; the honour, if not of being really in love with her, of being at least very near it, and saved only by her own indifference – (for still her resolution held of never marrying) – the honour, in short, of being marked out for her by all their joint acquaintance ... gave her to understand that Frank admired her extremely.

The Coles had been settled some years in Highbury, and were very good sort of people – friendly, liberal, and unpretending; but, on the other hand, they were of low origin, in trade, and only moderately genteel ... their love of society, and their new dining-room, prepared every body for their keeping dinner-company ... The regular and best families Emma could hardly suppose they would presume to invite ... Nothing should tempt her to go, if they did.

'... as they are so very desirous to have dear Emma dine with them, and as you will both be there, and Mr Knightley too, to take care of her, I cannot wish to prevent it ...'

She followed another carriage to Mr Cole's door; and was pleased to see that it was Mr Knightley's ... Emma had as much reason to be satisfied with the rest of the party as with Mr Knightley ... When the Westons arrived, the kindest looks of love, the strongest of admiration were for her, from both husband and wife; the son approached her with a cheerful eagerness, which marked her as his peculiar object, and at dinner she found him seated by her – and, as she firmly believed, not without some dexterity on his side.

... Frank Churchill. In he walked, the first and the handsomest; and after paying his compliments en passant to Miss Bates and her niece, made his way directly to the opposite side of the circle, where sat Miss Woodhouse; and till he could find a seat by her, would not sit at all. Emma divined what every body present must be thinking. She was his object, and every body must perceive it. She introduced him to her friend, Miss Smith.

'This is the luxury of a large party,' Mrs Weston said; – 'one can get near everybody, and say every thing. My dear Emma, I am longing to talk to you. I have been making discoveries and forming plans, just like yourself, and I must tell them while the idea is fresh. Do you know how Miss Bates and her niece came here? ... Mr Knightley's carriage had brought, and was to take them home again.'

' ... a suspicion darted into my head, and I have never been able to get it out again. The more I think of it, the more probable it appears. In short, I have made a match between Mr Knightley and Jane Fairfax. See the consequence of keeping you company! – What do you say to it?'

'Mr Knightley and Jane Fairfax!' exclaimed Emma. 'Dear Mrs Weston, how could you think of such a thing? – Mr Knightley! – Mr Knightley must not marry!'

Her objections to Mr Knightley's marrying did not in the least subside. She could see nothing but evil in it ... No, Mr Knightley must never marry.

... beginning an irresistible waltz; and Frank Churchill, coming up with most becoming gallantry to Emma, had secured her hand, and led her up to the top.

While waiting till the other young people could pair themselves off, Emma found time, in spite of the compliments she was receiving on her voice and her taste, to look about, and see what became of Mr Knightley.

' ... How did you think the Coxes looked?'

'Just as they always do – very vulgar.'

'They told me something,' said Harriet, rather hesitatingly, 'but it is nothing of any consequence.'

Emma was obliged to ask what they had told her, though fearful of its producing Mr Elton.

'They told me that Mr Martin dined with them last Saturday ... he was very agreeable the day he dined there.'

The appearance of the little sitting-room as they entered was tranquillity itself, Mrs Bates, deprived of her usual employment, slumbering on one side of the fire, Frank Churchill, at a table near her, most deedily occupied about her spectacles, and Jane Fairfax, standing with her back to them, intent on her pianoforte.

Busy as he was, however, the young man was yet able to shew a most happy countenance on seeing Emma again.

Miss Bates, passing near the window, descried Mr Knightley on horseback not far off.

'Mr Knightley, I declare! – I must speak to him if possible, just to thank him ... so obliged to you for the carriage last night.'

So began Miss Bates; and Mr Knightley seemed determined to be heard in his turn, for most resolutely and commandingly did he say,

'How is your niece, Miss Bates? – I want to inquire after you all, but particularly your niece. How is Miss Fairfax?'

... The listeners were amused; and Mrs Weston gave Emma a look of particular meaning.

It may be possible to do without dancing entirely. Instances have been known of young people passing many, many months successively, without being at any ball of any description, and no material injury accrue either to body or mind ...

'In short,' said Mr Churchill, 'perhaps, Miss Woodhouse – I think you can hardly be quite without suspicion' –

... It seemed like the forerunner of something absolutely serious, which she did not wish ... He stopt again, rose again, and seemed quite embarrassed. – He was more in love with her than Emma had supposed ...

A very friendly shake of the hand, a very earnest 'Goodbye,' closed the speech, and the door had soon shut out Frank Churchill. Short had been the notice – short their meeting; he was gone; and Emma felt so sorry to part, and foresaw so great a loss to their little society from his absence as to begin to be afraid of being too sorry, and feeling it too much.

... she could not doubt his having a decidedly warm admiration, a conscious preference of herself; and this persuasion, joined to all the rest, made her think that she must be a little in love with him, in spite of every previous determination against it.

'I certainly must,' said she. 'This sensation of listlessness, weariness, stupidity, this disinclination to sit down and employ myself, this feeling of every thing's being dull and insipid about the house! – I must be in love.'

'I shall do very well again after a little while.' ... Her resolution of refusal only grew more interesting by the addition of a scheme for Mr Churchill's subsequent consolation and happiness. His recollection of Harriet, and the words which clothed it, the 'beautiful little friend,' suggested to her the idea of Harriet's succeeding her in his affections. Was it impossible? – No ...

Mrs Elton was first seen at church: but though devotion might be interrupted, curiosity could not be satisfied by a bride in a pew, and it must be left for the visits in form which were then to be paid, to settle whether she were very pretty indeed, or only rather pretty, or not pretty at all ... Emma would not allow herself entirely to form an opinion of the lady ... she did not really like her.

She considered how peculiarly unlucky poor Mr Elton was in being in the same room at once with the woman he had just married, the woman he had wanted to marry, and the woman whom he had been expected to marry, she must allow him to have the right to look as little wise, and to be as much affectedly, and as little really easy as could be.

... the quarter of an hour quite convinced her that Mrs Elton was a vain woman, extremely well satisfied with herself, and thinking much of her own importance; that she meant to shine and be very superior, but the manners which had been formed in a bad school, pert and familiar; that all her notions were drawn from one set of people, and one style of living; that if not foolish she was ignorant, and that her society would certainly do Mr Elton no good.

'The advantages of Bath to the young are pretty generally understood. It would be a charming introduction for you, who have lived so secluded a life; and I could immediately secure you some of the best society in the place. A line from me would bring you a little host of acquaintance.'

... The idea of her being indebted to Mrs Elton for what was called an introduction – of her going into public under the auspices of a friend of Mrs Elton's ... The dignity of Miss Woodhouse, of Hartfield, was sunk indeed!

'Insufferable woman! ... worse than I had supposed. Absolutely insufferable! Knightley! – I could not have believed it. Knightley! – never seen him in her life before, and call him Knightley! – and discover that he is a gentleman ... all her airs of pert pretention and under-bred finery.'

In one respect Mrs Elton grew even worse than she had appeared at first. Her feelings altered towards Emma. – Offended, probably, by the little encouragement which her proposals of intimacy met with, she drew back in her turn and gradually became much more cold and distant ... Her manners, too – and Mr Elton's, were unpleasant towards Harriet. They were sneering and negligent.

Mr Knightley ... soon afterwards said,

'So you have been settling that I should marry Jane Fairfax?'

'No, indeed I have not. You have scolded me too much for match-making, for me to presume to take such a liberty with you ...'

'Jane Fairfax is a very charming young woman – but not even Jane Fairfax is perfect. She has a fault. She has not the open temper which a man would wish for in a wife.'

'Well, Mrs Weston,' said Emma, triumphantly when he left them, 'what do you say now to Mr Knightley's marrying Jane Fairfax?'

'Why really, dear Emma, I say that he is so very much occupied by the idea of not being in love with her, that I should not wonder if it were to end in his being so at last. Do not beat me.'

'I did not mean, I was not thinking of the slave-trade,' replied Jane; 'governess-trade, I assure you, was all that I had in view ... But I only mean to say that there are advertising offices, and that by applying to them I should have no doubt of very soon meeting with something that would do.'

'I know you, I know you; you would take up with any thing; but I shall be a little more nice, and I am sure the good Campbells will be quite on my side; with your superior talents, you have a right to move in the first circle.'

'I am very serious in not wishing any thing to be attempted at present for me. I am exceedingly obliged to you, Mrs Elton, I am obliged to any body who feels for me, but I am quite serious in wishing nothing to be done till the summer ...'

Mr Weston gave her a letter, it was from Frank [Churchill], and to herself; [Mr Weston] had met with it in his way, and had taken the liberty of opening it.

'Read it, read it,' said he, 'it will give you pleasure; only a few lines – will not take you long; read it to Emma.'

The two ladies looked over it together ...

'Well, he is coming, you see; good news, I think.'

A very little quiet reflection was enough to satisfy Emma as to the nature of her agitation on hearing this news of Frank Churchill. She was soon convinced that it was not for herself she was feeling at all apprehensive or embarrassed; it was for him. Her own attachment had really subsided into a mere nothing it was not worth thinking of.

One good thing was immediately brought to a certainty ... the ball at the Crown. It had not been forgotten before, but it had been soon acknowledged vain to attempt to fix a day. Now, however, it was absolutely to be ... Mr Weston's ball was to be a real thing. A very few to-morrows stood between the young people of Highbury and happiness.

No misfortune occurred, again to prevent the ball. The day approached, the day arrived ... Frank Churchill seemed to have been on the watch; and though he did not say much, his eyes declared that he meant to have a delightful evening ... Frank was standing by Emma, but not steadily; there was a restlessness, which showed a mind not at ease. He was looking about, he was going to the door, he was watching for the sound of other carriages, impatient to begin ...

Mrs Elton then said,

'Nobody can think less of dress in general than I do – but upon such an occasion as this, when every body's eyes are so much upon me, and in compliment to the Westons – who I have no doubt are giving this ball chiefly to do me honour – I would not wish to be inferior to others. And I see very few pearls in the room except mine.'

It had just occurred to Mrs Weston that Mrs Elton must be asked to begin the ball; that she would expect it; which interfered with all their wishes of giving Emma that distinction. – Emma heard the sad truth with fortitude.

Mr Weston and Mrs Elton led the way, Mr Frank Churchill and Miss Woodhouse followed. Emma must submit to stand second to Mrs Elton, though she had always considered the ball as peculiarly for her. It was almost enough to make her think of marrying.

She was more disturbed by Mr Knightley's not dancing than by any thing else. – There he was, among the standers-by, where he ought not to be; he ought to be dancing ... Whenever she caught his eye, she forced him to smile; but in general he was looking grave ... he seemed often observing her.

The last two dances before supper were begun, and Harriet had no partner; – the only young lady sitting down ... But Emma's wonder lessened soon afterwards, on seeing Mr Elton sauntering about. He would not ask Harriet to dance if it were possible to be avoided ... He came to the part of the room where the sitters-by were collected, spoke to some, and walked about in front of them, as if to show his liberty ... The kind-hearted, gentle Mrs Weston had left her seat to join him and say, 'Do not you dance, Mr Elton?' to which his prompt reply was, 'Most readily, Mrs Weston, if you will dance with me.'

' ... but there is a young lady disengaged whom I should be very glad to see dancing – Miss Smith.'

'Miss Smith – oh! – I had not observed. – You are extremely obliging – and if I were not an old married man. – But my dancing days are over Mrs Weston ...'

... Emma looked round for a moment; he had joined Mr Knightley at a little distance, and was arranging himself for settled conversation, while smiles of high glee passed between him and his wife ... In another moment a happier sight caught her; – Mr Knightley leading Harriet to the set!

'They aimed at wounding more than Harriet,' said he. 'Emma, why is it they are your enemies? ... but confess, Emma, that you did want him to marry Harriet.'

'I did,' replied Emma, 'and they cannot forgive me.'

' ... in return for your acknowledging so much, I will do you the justice to say, that you would have chosen for him better than he has chosen for himself. – Harriet Smith has some first-rate qualities, which Mrs Elton is totally without.'

'Whom are you going to dance with?' asked Mr Knightley.

She hesitated a moment, and then replied, 'With you, if you will ask me,'

'Will you?' said he, offering his hand.

'Indeed I will.'

Frank Churchill with Harriet leaning on his arm – actually Harriet! A moment sufficed to convince her that something extraordinary had happened. Harriet looked white and frightened ... they were all three soon in the hall, and Harriet immediately sinking into a chair fainted away.

Harriet was soon assailed by half a dozen children, headed by a stout woman and a great boy, all clamorous, and impertinent in look ... More and more frightened, she immediately promised them money, and taking out her purse, gave them a shilling, and begged them not to want more, or to use her ill ... In this state Frank Churchill had found her, she trembling and conditioning, they loud and insolent.

Such an adventure as this, – a fine young man and a lovely young woman thrown together in such a way, could hardly fail of suggesting certain ideas to the coldest heart and the steadiest brain. So Emma thought, at least.

'Oh! Miss Woodhouse, believe me, I have not the presumption to suppose – indeed I am not so mad. – But it is a pleasure to me to admire him at a distance – and to think of his infinite superiority to all the rest of the world, with the gratitude, wonder, and veneration, which are so proper, in me especially.'

Mr Knightley, who, for some reason best known to himself, had certainly taken an early dislike to Frank Churchill, was only growing to dislike him more. He began to suspect him of some double dealing in his pursuit of Emma ... but while so many were devoting him to Emma, and Emma herself making him over to Harriet, Mr Knightley began to suspect him of some inclination to trifle with Jane Fairfax.

'My dear Emma,' said he at last, with earnest kindness, 'do you think you perfectly understand the degree of acquaintance between the gentleman and lady we have been speaking of?'

'Between Mr Frank Churchill and Miss Fairfax? Oh! yes, perfectly. – Why do you make a doubt of it?'

'Have you never at any time had reason to think that he admired her, or that she admired him?'

'Never, never!'

In this walk Emma and Mr Weston found all the others assembled; and towards this view she immediately perceived Mr Knightley and Harriet distinct from the rest, quietly leading the way. Mr Knightley and Harriet! – It was an odd tête-à-tête; but she was glad to see it.

Jane Fairfax appeared, coming quickly in from the garden, and with a look of escape. Little expecting to meet Miss Woodhouse so soon, there was a start at first ...

'Will you be so kind,' she said, 'when I am missed, as to say that I am gone home? – I am going this moment ... the greatest kindness you can show me, will be to let me have my own way, and only say that I am gone when it is necessary.'

They had a very fine day for Box Hill ... The Eltons walked together; Mr Knightley took charge of Miss Bates and Jane; and Emma and Harriet belonged to Frank Churchill. And Mr Weston tried, in vain to make them harmonize better.

'Our companions are exceedingly stupid. What shall we do to rouse them? Any nonsense will serve. They shall talk. Ladies and gentlemen, I am ordered by Miss Woodhouse (who, wherever she is, presides,) to say, that she desires to know what you are all thinking of?'

Some laughed, and answered good-humouredly. Miss Bates said a great deal; Mrs Elton swelled at the idea of Miss Woodhouse's presiding ...

' ... she only demands from each of you either one thing very clever, be it prose or verse, original or repeated or two things moderately clever or three things very dull indeed, and she engages to laugh heartily at them all.'

'Oh! very well,' exclaimed Miss Bates, 'then I need not be uneasy. "Three things very dull indeed." That will just do for me, you know.'

Emma could not resist.

'Ah! ma'am, but there may be a difficulty. Pardon me – but you will be limited as to number – only three at once.'

While waiting for the carriage, she found Mr Knightley by her side ...

'Emma, I must once more speak to you as I have been used to do: a privilege rather endured than allowed, perhaps, but I must still use it. I cannot see you acting wrong, without a remonstrance. How could you be so unfeeling to Miss Bates? How could you be so insolent in your wit to a woman of her character, age, and situation! – Emma, I had not thought it possible.'

'Oh!' cried Emma, 'I know there is not a better creature in the world: but you must allow, that what is good and what is ridiculous are most unfortunately blended in her.'

The wretchedness of a scheme to Box Hill was in Emma's thoughts all the evening ... In the warmth of true contrition, she would call upon Miss Bates the very next morning, and it should be the beginning on her side, of a regular, equal, kindly intercourse.

'Where – may I ask – is Miss Fairfax going?'

'To a Mrs Smallridge – charming woman – most superior – to have the charge of her three little girls – delightful children ...'

'Mrs Elton, I suppose, has been the person to whom Miss Fairfax owes – '

'Yes, our good Mrs Elton. The most indefatigable, true friend. She would not take a denial.'

' ... And when is Miss Fairfax to leave you?'

'Very soon, very soon indeed; that's the worst of it. Within a fortnight.'

Emma's pensive meditations, as she walked home, were not interrupted; but on entering the parlour, she found those who must rouse her. Mr Knightley and Harriet had arrived during her absence, and were sitting with her father. – Mr Knightley immediately got up and, in a manner decidedly graver than usual, said,

'I would not go away without seeing you, but I have not time to spare, and therefore must now be gone directly. I am going to London, to spend a few days with John and Isabella.'

One morning ... Emma was called down stairs to Mr Weston ... He met her at the parlour door, and hardly asking her how she did, in the natural key of his voice, sunk it immediately, to say, unheard by her father,

'Can you come to Randalls at any time this morning? – Do, if it be possible. Mrs Weston wants to see you. She must see you.'

'Mr Frank Churchill has been here this very morning, on a most extraordinary errand. It is impossible to express our surprise. He came to speak to his father on a subject, – to announce an attachment ... More than an attachment, indeed ...an engagement – a positive engagement. – What will you say, Emma – what will any body say, when it is known that Frank Churchill and Miss Fairfax are engaged; – nay, that they have been long engaged?'

'I will farther tell you, that there was a period in the early part of our acquaintance, when I did like him, when I was very much disposed to be attached to him – nay, was attached – and how it came to cease, is perhaps the wonder ...'

' ... It was our darling wish that you might be attached to each other – and we were persuaded that it was so. – Imagine what we have been feeling on your account.'

' ... it has sunk him in my opinion.'

' ... Me!' cried Harriet, colouring, and astonished, 'Why should you caution me? – you do not think I care about Mr Frank Churchill.'

' ... Let us understand each other now, without the possibility of farther mistake. Are you speaking of – Mr Knightley?'

'To be sure I am ... I thought you knew.'

'Good God!' cried Emma, 'this has been a most unfortunate – most deplorable mistake! – What is to be done? ... Have you any idea of Mr Knightley's returning your affection?'

'Yes,' replied Harriet modestly, but not fearfully – 'I must say that I have.'

Why was it so much worse that Harriet should be in love with Mr Knightley, than with Frank Churchill? Why was the evil so dreadfully increased by Harriet's having some hope of a return? It darted through her, with the speed of an arrow, that Mr Knightley must marry no one but herself!

'Is not it possible, that when enquiring, as you thought, into the state of your affections, he might be alluding to Mr Martin – he might have Mr Martin's interest in view?' – But Harriet rejected the suspicion with spirit.

'Mr Martin! No, indeed! – There was not a hint of Mr Martin – I hope I know better now, than to care for Mr Martin, or to be suspected of it.'

'Harriet, I will only venture to declare, that Mr Knightley is the last man in the world, who would intentionally give any woman the idea of his feeling for her more than he really does.'

To understand, thoroughly understand her own heart, was the first endeavour ... How long had Mr Knightley been so dear to her, as every feeling declared him now to be? Till now that she was threatened with its loss, Emma had never known how much of her happiness depended on being first with Mr Knightley, first in interest and affection. – Satisfied that it was so, and feeling it her due, she had enjoyed it without reflection; and only in the dread of being supplanted, found how inexpressibly important it had been.

Could she be secure of ... his never marrying at all, she believed she should be perfectly satisfied. – Let him but continue the same Mr Knightley to her and her father, the same Mr Knightley to all the world.

She saw Mr Knightley passing through the garden door, and coming towards her, – It was the first intimation of his being returned from London. She had been thinking of him the moment before ... She must be collected and calm.

'You have some news to hear, now you are come back, that will rather surprise you.'

'If you mean Miss Fairfax and Frank Churchill, I have heard that already.'

'You probably have been less surprised than any of us, for you have had your suspicions. – I have not forgotten that you once tried to give me a caution ...'

'Time, my dearest Emma, time will heal the wound.'

'You are very kind – but you are mistaken – and I must set you right. I am not in want of that sort of compassion.'

'Emma, I must tell what you will not ask, though I may wish it unsaid the next moment.'

He was wishing to confide in her – perhaps to consult her; – cost her what it would, she would listen.

'I stopped you ungraciously, just now, Mr Knightley, and, I am afraid, gave you pain. – But if you have any wish to speak openly to me as a friend, or to ask my opinion of any thing that you may have in contemplation – as a friend, indeed, you may command me. – I will hear whatever you like. I will tell you exactly what I think.'

'I cannot make speeches, Emma:' – he soon resumed; and in a tone of such sincere, decided, intelligible tenderness as was tolerably convincing. – 'If I loved you less, I might be able to talk about it more. But you know what I am. – You hear nothing but truth from me ... At present, I ask only to hear, once to hear your voice.'

This half hour had given to each the same precious certainty of being beloved, had cleared from each the same degree of ignorance, jealousy, or distrust.

She would have been too happy but for poor Harriet; but every blessing of her own seemed to involve and advance the sufferings of her friend ... and it really was too much to hope even of Harriet, that she could be in love with more than three men in one year.

'You are prepared for the worst, I see – and very bad it is. Harriet Smith marries Robert Martin.'

' ... It is not that such a circumstance would now make me unhappy, but I cannot believe it. It seems an impossibility ... I am perfectly satisfied,' replied Emma, with the brightest smiles, 'and most sincerely wish them happy.'

The wedding was very much like other weddings, where the parties have no taste for finery or parade; and Mrs Elton, from the particulars detailed by her husband, thought it all extremely shabby and very inferior to her own. – 'Very little white satin, very few lace veils; a most pitiful business!'

Published by Museum Quilts (UK) Inc.
254-258 Goswell Road, London EC1V 7EB

ISBN: 1 897954 83 2

Printed and bound in Hong Kong